Surfmen and Lifesavers

Surfmen and Lifesavers

by Paul Giambarba

Including
Heroes of the Life Saving Service
from *The Century* Magazine, April 1898

The Scrimshaw Press

Centerville, Cape Cod, MA 02632-0010

Revised edition 1985

Library of Congress Catalog Card No. 67-20238

ISBN 0-87155-117-9

Printed in the United States of America

Contents

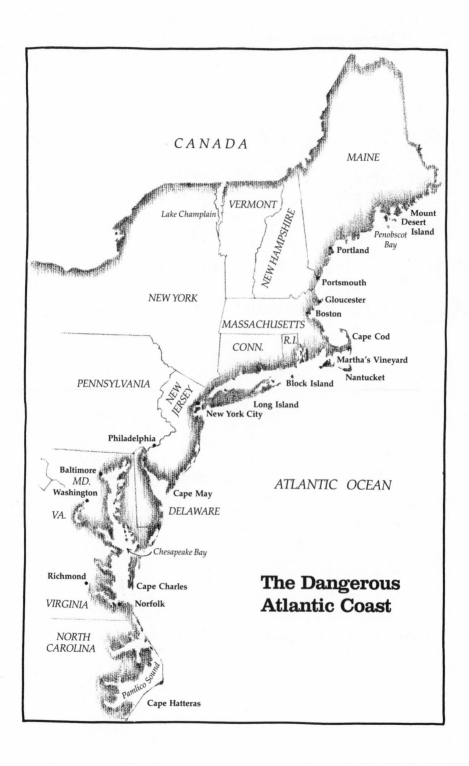

CANADA

MAINE

VERMONT

Lake Champlain

NEW HAMPSHIRE

Mount
Desert
Island

Penobscot Bay

Portland

NEW YORK

Portsmouth

Gloucester

Boston

MASSACHUSETTS

Cape Cod

CONN.

R.I.

Martha's Vineyard

Nantucket

PENNSYLVANIA

NEW JERSEY

Block Island

Long Island

New York City

Philadelphia

Baltimore

MD.

Washington

VA.

Cape May

DELAWARE

ATLANTIC OCEAN

Chesapeake Bay

Richmond

Cape Charles

VIRGINIA

Norfolk

NORTH
CAROLINA

Pamlico Sound

Cape Hatteras

The Dangerous
Atlantic Coast

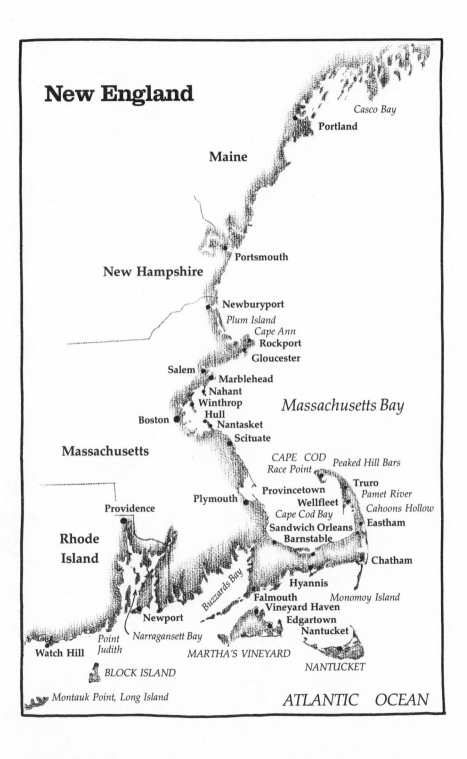

New England

Maine

Casco Bay
Portland

Portsmouth

New Hampshire

Newburyport
Plum Island
Cape Ann
Rockport
Gloucester
Salem
Marblehead
Nahant
Winthrop   *Massachusetts Bay*
Hull
Boston   Nantasket
Scituate

Massachusetts

CAPE COD   *Peaked Hill Bars*
Race Point
Truro
Provincetown   *Pamet River*
Plymouth   Wellfleet   *Cahoons Hollow*
Cape Cod Bay   Eastham
Sandwich Orleans
Providence   Barnstable

Rhode   Chatham
Island
Hyannis

Falmouth   *Monomoy Island*
Newport   Vineyard Haven
Buzzards Bay   Edgartown
Nantucket
Point   *Narragansett Bay*
Watch Hill   *Judith*   *MARTHA'S VINEYARD*
NANTUCKET
BLOCK ISLAND

Montauk Point, Long Island   *ATLANTIC OCEAN*

1   Surfmen and Lifesavers

Ship in distress!

Sam Fisher

SUPPOSE you are Surfman Sam Fisher. Samuel O. Fisher of Provincetown, Massachusetts, where the Pilgrims first landed. You were born the year the Civil War began, 1861. You are nineteen years old and a member of the United States Lifesaving Service at the Peaked Hill Bars Station at the tip of Cape Cod. Sailors say that the Peaked Hill Bars are the most dangerous stretch of shore along the New England Coast.

Your job as a surfman is to patrol the beaches and to pull the midship oar in the rescue or "surfboat." On patrol, especially on stormy nights, you scan the horizon for ships in distress, walking the beach while the wind batters you unmercifully. The sand stings your face and eyes. You are soaked to the skin, cold and miserable. Through the murk you see the outline of rigging, the masts of a vessel that has struck—gone aground—on the bars. You light your red flare, the "Coston signal," to let the stricken crew know they have been seen. You struggle back to the station through the soft sand dunes. Every difficult step you take is a matter of life or death to the shipwrecked crew out on the bars. The other surfmen also race back from their posts after seeing the flare, fighting their way through the storm and the sand.

Hauling the surfboat

At the station the station keeper, or captain, orders the equipment to the beach. You and the other surfmen pull the huge surfboat and the lifesaving equipment out of the boat house, down the ramp and over the bank to the edge of the sea. There, through howling gale winds and roaring surf, you launch the boat. A huge wave strikes it, turns it end over end. You launch it again. Another wave fills it to the gunwales. You return to the beach, empty out the boat, launch it again and again—until you've overcome the surf of the shore break. The stricken vessel is out too far to be reached by shooting a line to it. The crew can only be saved by boat. You must row out to them and bring them back.

[15]

Through the storm you strain at the oar, pulling for your life. At the wreck you see the broken spars flailed by the wind, wreckage from the ship is tossed about by the waves. You think about the frail cedar-planked surfboat and how quickly it could be stove in. The crew of the wreck is in the rigging begging to be saved. The station keeper, Captain Atkins, at the steering oar shouts encouragement to them, commands them to jump in the water. You pull them out of the water and into the boat—one by one—in spite of the thunderous waves, the flailing spars, the wind and their panic. Somehow you get them, the boat, and yourself to shore.

Is this an unusual occurrence? Not at all. This is what you are trained to do for a little more than a dollar a day. The unofficial motto of your service is "You have to go out—you don't have to come back." As a surfman at Peaked Hill Bars and then as keeper of the Race Point Station, Provincetown, you will cheat death many times in many different ways. Over a hundred vessels will have met disaster while you are at your station. Over six hundred souls will be at the point of death and at the mercy of the seas. You and your crew will save almost all of them.

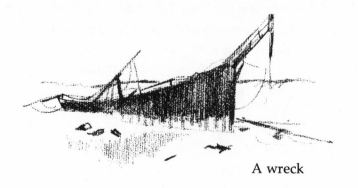

A wreck

"Wreck ahoy!"

It is the night of November 29, 1880. A sloop, *C. E. Trumbull,* with a crew of six is being battered by a howling northwest wind. By 4 A.M. the sloop is stranded on the Peaked Hill Bars just east of the lifesaving station. Surfman Charles Kelley and you are on duty outside the station. Against the black sky you see the faint glow of the sloop's lights.

"Look, Sam, there's something out there!"

The banging you hear is the canvas and rigging slapping in the wind. You race to the beach. You see the vessel out on the bar being battered by the waves. Kelley lights his Coston signal. Whoosh! You are both bathed in the light of the brilliant red flare.

You sprint back to the station. The rest of the crew—Taylor, Mayo, Cole, Young and Captain Atkins—have seen the flare and are alerted. Captain Atkins has commanded the surfboat to be launched. With Taylor, Mayo, Young, Kelley and the Captain you launch the boat easily; the surf at the beach is not high.

At the bar, where the *Trumbull* lies foundering, the sea is rough and dangerous. There she is now, Taylor throws a line aboard her. Somebody up on deck makes it fast. Captain Atkins orders you to haul up on the line. The boat edges close to the wreck. One of the sailors on board tosses his seabag into the surfboat. Captain Atkins calls out, "We're not here for your baggage; get yourselves in the boat."

Four men are taken off and are safely ashore in a matter of minutes. You return to the wreck, through the same dangerous sea for the two remaining seamen. Taylor stands in the bow of the boat, the heaving line coiled in his hand. The *Trumbull* is rolling and pitching, the main boom slatting.

"Look out for the boom, Cap'n," shouts Young, who is about to make fast to the *Trumbull* with the boat hook.

A rising wave causes the *Trumbull* to roll to leeward and the boom pitches into the water. When the vessel rolls to windward the boom comes up under the surfboat and catches on its outer flotation belt of cork, tipping it over.

[18]

Disaster strikes

As the boat rolls over you are caught by some rope. You can hardly keep your head out of water. You summon all the strength you can muster and break out of the tangle in a desperate lunge. You crawl on the upturned boat. The others are all there except for Taylor who is hurt. You see him in the water. He is groaning. You grab him, drag him up on the boat. A big wave strikes and he loses his hold. Young reaches out for him and helps him back on. Together, all of you tug on one side of the boat and it is righted. You get in, but in less than a minute another wave rolls the boat bottom up again.

You have a firm hold on the overturned boat. You see Captain Atkins and stick out your leg. He grabs your foot and pulls himself to the boat. Another huge wave and you are separated again. Taylor is nearby calling for help. He clutches at you for support in the water. All that he reaches are the strings of your life jacket and these give way. He disappears from sight in the furious sea. You are alone in the cold choppy water, hundreds of yards from shore. You decide to swim for it.

Luckily you make shore, but you have drifted two miles from the station. You stagger toward its light. There you get dry clothes and the medicinal brandy. You revive, summon all your strength once more and go out again. You help bring in Kelley who has also swum ashore. Now he is unconscious. With others, you help revive him. Then you go on down the beach where you find the body of Captain Atkins.* You meet another surfman from another station and he tells you that Taylor and Mayo have drowned, too. You feel very tired and you head back for the station but it is hard to move your feet. You just sit down in the sand in the cold November night and soon others come along and help you back.   * For another account of this tragedy, see Appendix.

Exhausted

Ephraim S. Dyer

Sam Fisher's experience was not unique. Just a few miles south of Provincetown at the Pamet River Station in Truro, the No. 1 (highest in rank) Surfman Ephraim S. Dyer was still serving as a lifesaver in 1902 at the age of 57, after thirty years of narrow escapes in the performance of his duty. In that time he assisted at all the wrecks that took place in this dangerous area.

On January 3, 1878, the triple wreck of the *Addie P. Avery, Powwow* and *Miles Standish* occurred. Surfman Dyer was trapped in the wreckage of one of the vessels and dragged to the bottom by a rope tangled about his legs. He was saved when one of his fellow surfmen rushed in from shore with a knife and cut Dyer free. But in all his years of lifesaving this hardy soul suffered nothing more than a sprained ankle.

The beach patrol at some stations was equally dangerous. When the tide was high, surfmen were driven to the tops of the dunes and had to make their way in the darkness perched at times one hundred feet above the roaring surf. Some, like William Francis, were caught by huge waves and carried out to sea by undertow. William Paine's eyes were frozen shut during a freezing snowstorm. Miraculously, both men survived.

Who were these valiant lifesavers? Usually they were hardy local boys who were experienced boatmen and strong swimmers. Obviously they were as courageous as anyone could hope to be. Because of their dedication to duty, their willingness to lay down their own lives to save others, a truly amazing number of people were saved from death at sea. In the forty-four years from 1871 until it became part of the United States Coast Guard in 1915, the United States Life Saving Service went to the aid of 178,741 persons in distress. 177,286 were saved!

Emblem of the Life Saving Service

Dirty weather

How it all Began—

Bad weather has always made life at sea miserable and often put man's life in danger. Anyone who has been out in a boat knows how important it is to come ashore quickly if a storm develops. A sudden summer squall can come up quickly and turn the calm surface of the water into a deadly chop. Today a boat with a good motor can usually get to shore safely in a storm if the boat's skipper is careful and capable. Large vessels out in the open sea have many helpful aids for safe navigation. They take their bearings by radio signals beamed at them from shore. They use radar screens to look for obstacles in their path that can be far away through fog and darkness. Radio weather reports tell them when a storm is due, the direction it will take, the probable force of its winds and the condition of the sea.

Most of the ships that sail the seas today can ride out the worst kind of hurricane and typhoon.

Years ago, however, it was much different. The old sailing vessels were apt to find themselves in trouble if caught in a storm off shore. The wind would tear their sails to shreds. The force of wind and water against the vessel would cause the heavy anchor chains to snap, and the ships would be dashed against the shore. Steamships also met with disaster in storms. The most memorable one in New England was the steamer *City of Portland* which sailed for

Portland, Maine, from Boston on November 26, 1898 and was lost at sea the next morning. One hundred and ninety-one passengers and crew members perished in the violent storm of November 26 and 27, which many have called ever since "the great Portland Storm of 1898." No rescue was possible because the *Portland* went to pieces in Cape Cod Bay miles from shore. No one was saved.

City of Portland

2   Early Disasters

An early victim

After thousands of lives and countless ships were lost, the United States government began a lifesaving service to patrol the coast on the lookout for vessels in trouble. We can only guess at the number of shipwrecks which might have taken place off the New England shores from the time of the Pilgrims to the establishment of the United States Life Saving Service in 1871. Only the greatest disasters were written into town records and histories until the government began printing reports each year. Most of the storms were unrecorded also. The hurricane of August 14-15, 1635 is the first important one to be written about. Gale winds and 20-foot tides brought death and destruction to the Indians and early settlers. Most of their few precious vessels were damaged or wrecked off Nova Scotia and the New England coast.

Nine years earlier, in 1626, the first shipwreck on Cape Cod was recorded. This was the little ship *Sparrow Hawk*, with colonists from England bound for Virginia. *Sparrow Hawk*'s passengers all escaped because the ship was not badly damaged. The remains of this vessel may be seen at Pilgrim Hall, Plymouth.

Sparrowhawk foundering on the bars

Earlier disasters surely took place. When Bartholomew Gosnold entered New England waters in 1602, he was met by Indians in a boat of the type used by fishermen from the Bay of Biscay between France and Spain. This boat may have been lost by Biscayan fishermen who were fishing off the North American shore.

While little is known about early shipwrecks, even less is known about rescues. Most of the lifesaving attempts were made by men who have remained unknown. Often, the keeper of a lighthouse would come to the aid of a vessel in distress and take off as many people as he could safely manage. This was the case when a Boston brigantine broke up on the rocks near Boston Light in the southeast gale of December 4, 1768.

On the same day eighteen years later, a British brig *Lucretia* was wrecked on Point Shirley, Winthrop, during a heavy snowstorm which brought very high tides. Many of the crew who got safely to shore were frozen to death in the snow. Four days later on Friday, December 8, another severe snowstorm fell and brought a greater tragedy to Boston Harbor. A schooner was driven ashore on Lovell's Island and all on board were lost.

In the Christmas storm of 1778, seventy-four persons froze to death when the brig *General Arnold* went aground on the sand flats off Plymouth harbor. Only the gallant efforts of the Plymouth townsfolk kept the loss from being greater. In below-zero weather, against an icy, driving wind, the men of Plymouth inched their way across the ice toward the *General Arnold*. They pushed timbers and planks ahead of themselves and built a rescue track to the stricken vessel.

When the Plymouth rescuers finally reached the ship on the morning of December 26, they could hardly believe their eyes. It was hard to tell the living from the dead. Barnabas Downes, of Barnstable, heard the rescuers speak of him as dead. He was so frozen that he could not move his arms or legs or cry out. All that he could do was move his eyes. Fortunately, one of the rescuers noticed this. Downes was taken, with the other survivors, to a home and placed in a tank of cold water to thaw out. Although this method brought terrible pain to the frozen parts of the body, it saved the lives of the few who were lucky enough to survive.

Nine more died within a week of the disaster, but fifteen became completely well again in time. These survivors owed their lives to the heroic efforts of the ordinary towns-people of Plymouth who came to their rescue.

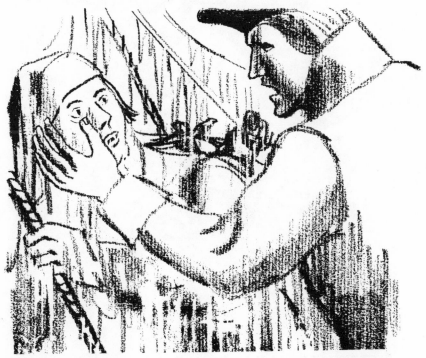

Barnabas Downes

In the United States, in 1786, all lifesaving was being done by ordinary citizens acting on their own. The Massachusetts Humane Society awarded its first prize of 28 shillings in February, 1786 to Andrew Sloane. Sloane had saved a little boy from drowning who had fallen through thin ice. The Society first began a program of building shelters along the coast. These were to aid the survivors of wrecks who had safely made their way to shore, only to perish in the storm looking for a place of refuge.

Seven years later, in 1785, four men met in Boston to

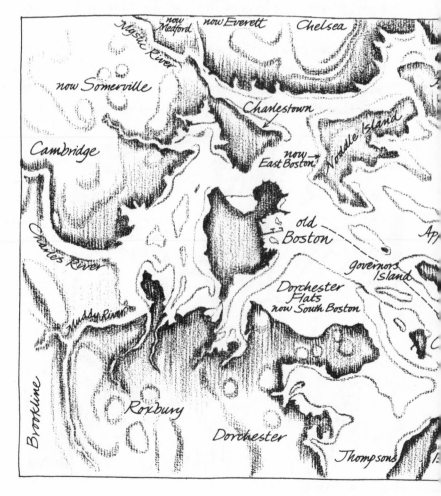

find a way to save the lives of those who might be shipwrecked along the New England coast. In this way the Massachusetts Humane Society was born.

The first meeting took place on State Street in Boston at the Bunch of Grapes Tavern on January 5, 1786. It was very much like British and Dutch societies begun in Holland in 1767 and England in 1774. The first organized lifesaving effort must be credited to the Chinese, however. It began in 1737 with five lifeboats to aid people in peril from floods and typhoons off the China Sea.

BOSTON HARBOR
about 1775
showing sand flats
and
shipping channels *N*

now
Winthrop

Shirley gut

Point Shirley

Deer Island

and
acle I. Long I. Nix's Mate Lovells I.

Gallops I.

Georges I. Nantasket Beach

Hull gut Pt. Allerton

Rainsford I. Peddocks I. Hull

The first shelters were built on Lovell's Island in Boston Harbor, at Scituate Beach, and Nantasket Beach. Ninety-two such shelters were eventually built by the Society along the Massachusetts coast. By 1845 the Massachusetts Humane Society had eighteen lifesaving stations as well as many simple shelters along the dangerous coast. The stations were equipped with rescue boats and mortars for shooting life lines aboard stricken vessels.

The ten years from 1841 to 1851 were a time of bad storms and many disasters. The Massachusetts Humane Society did what it could, with its crude huts and volunteer crews of lifesavers. And fearless citizens of coastal towns risked their own lives time and time again to save the crew of a vessel in trouble offshore.

There was obviously a great need for a government rescue service which would extend along the entire Atlantic coastline. Finally, in 1847, Congress voted $5,000 to assist the shipwrecked. The money was not spent. In 1848, $10,000 was set aside to build eight boathouses on the New Jersey shore—another dangerous stretch of coast. The $5,000 voted in 1847 was given to the Massachusetts Humane Society to build and equip more stations along the Massachusetts coast. In New Jersey the funds were wasted. The badly equipped boathouses were not cared for and the keys to the huts were left at the nearest private home.

By 1850 Congress had spent $40,000 for lifesaving stations on Long Island, New Jersey, and only one in New England—at Watch Hill, the most westerly point of the Rhode Island coast.

3   The Government Effort

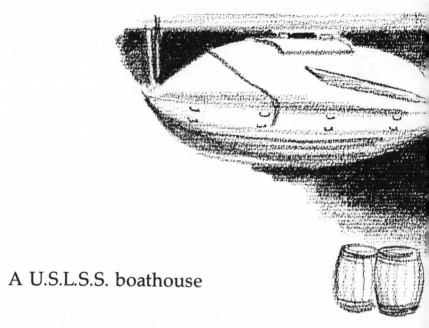

A U.S.L.S.S. boathouse

More and more money was voted by Congress. Soon there were one hundred and thirty-seven lifeboats on duty along the United States coasts—fifty-five of them at the New York and New Jersey shores. Even with all this money, the government effort soon became a mess. There were no properly trained crews. Many of the men put in charge of the stations were chosen for their friendship with the important people of their time rather than their ability. Equipment was stolen, left to rot.

In 1853, three hundred people were lost on the coast of New Jersey in the wreck of the *Powhatan*. This aroused so many people that Congress had to do something about its badly run lifesaving service. A superintendent was put in charge of the whole service, boathouse keepers were named and paid a salary. The stations and equipment were put in working order. But it was not enough. There was still nothing done about stationing trained crews of lifesavers at the stations.

In 1869, a bill in Congress that called for crews at these stations was voted down. Instead, Congress voted for crews at every other station. As a result, only half the posts were manned.

The winter of 1870-1871 was one of the worst of all for wrecks along the coast. No one could shut his eyes to the need for a proper lifesaving service to be run by the federal government. The coast was not guarded as it should be. The service was not as good as it had to be to save lives. In more than twenty years, Congress had only done part of the job that needed to be done. Finally, some steps were taken and progress was made.

First of all, $200,000 was voted to pay for crews of surfmen to patrol the beach and man the surfboats. In the early days of the service these men were paid wages of $40 per month.

Then, Sumner I. Kimball was moved from his post as director of the Revenue Marine Service to take over the Life Saving Service. The Revenue Marine Service, which guarded against smugglers, became the Revenue Cutter Service in 1863 and together, with the Life Saving Service, became the United States Coast Guard in 1915. Kimball sent officers of the Marine Service to the lifesaving stations to report on what they found there.

It may seem hard to believe but they found the same mess that had existed twenty years before. Some stations were in ruin. Some had no equipment. In many places anything that wasn't nailed down had been stolen. Orders were not obeyed. The money that Congress had voted had been wasted again.

Now, in 1872, the time had finally come for action. Station keepers who were useless were sent packing. Their posts were filled by skilled boatmen, instead of men with friends in public office. The crews were made up of good swimmers and strong men who knew their way around boats and boat gear. It was no problem to find these men; in every town along the coast there were many lads of eighteen who had been going to sea for ten years and more.

Beach patrols were begun. The surfmen walked posts along the shore, looking for vessels in danger. New stations were built—two more in Rhode Island and nine on Cape Cod. These were the first for the Cape, one of the worst stretches of coast along the entire Atlantic seaboard. Four more Cape stations were added later.

4 A Typical United States Life Saving Station

Boathouse and living quarters

A station kitchen

J. W. Dalton, in "Life Savers of Cape Cod," published at Sandwich, Massachusetts, in 1902 tells about these stations as they were at that time.

"The life-saving stations on Cape Cod are situated among the sand hills common to the eastern shores of the Cape, at distances back from the high-water mark to ensure their safety. In most instances they are plain structures, designed to serve as a home for the crew and to afford storage for the boats and other apparatus. In most of the stations on Cape Cod the lower floor is divided into five rooms—a kitchen, a keeper's room, a boat and beach apparatus room. Wide double-leafed doors with a sloping platform permit the quick and easy running out of the surf-boat and other apparatus from the station.

"The second storey contains two rooms; one the sleeping room for the crew; the other has spare cots for rescued persons, and is also used as a storeroom.

"On every station there is a lookout or observatory, from which the life savers, during the day when the weather is fair, keep a careful watch of all shipping along the coast. In order that the life-saving stations may be distinguished from a long distance at sea, they are usually painted dark red, and as a further aid to shipping, they are marked by a flagstaff about 60 feet high erected close by them. This flagstaff is also used to signal passing vessels by the International code. These stations are manned from the 1st of August until June 1st following, the keeper remaining on

Sounding a warning

duty throughout the year. The stations are generally furnished with two surf-boats (supplied with oars, life-preservers, life-boat compass, drag, boat-hooks, hatchet, heaving line, knife, bucket, and other outfits), boat carriages, two sets of breeches-buoy apparatus (including guns and accessories), carts for the transportation of the apparatus, a life-car, cork jackets (life-preservers), Coston signals, signal rockets, signal flags of the International and General signal code, medicine chest with contents, patrol lanterns, barometer, thermometer, patrol clocks, the requisite furniture (for housekeeping by the crew and for the succor of rescued persons), fuel, oil, tools for the repair of the boats and apparatus, and minor repairs to the buildings, and the necessary books and stationery.''

Signal flags

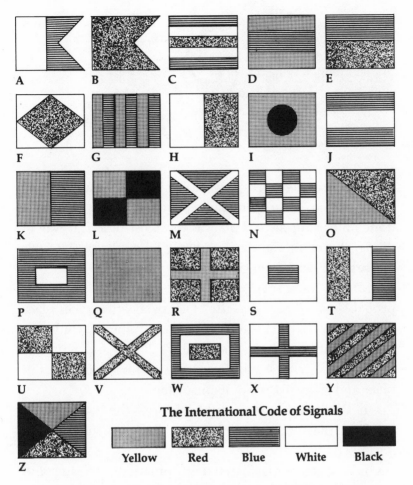

The International Code of Signals

Yellow	Red	Blue	White	Black

The signal flags were used to send messages to vessels at sea. Sometimes these ships would want only to know their positions, the correct latitude and longitude. Or they might be in need of something other than rescue—and could signal for whatever they might need.

The stations were connected by telephone. Shipping passing by the shore was kept under close watch by telephone talk among stations. In the case of emergencies help was quickly rushed from other stations.

The lifesaving work week began just after Sunday midnight, or 0001 hours Monday morning. Certain tasks were done on certain days. This was the most practical way of doing chores in the days of hand labor, before electric motors and gasoline engines.

Mondays were spent putting the station in order. This probably was the same as the "G.I. party" that takes place in military barracks today. All equipment would be cleaned and polished, the station's floors and windows washed, the surfmen's uniforms and personal effects put in place and arranged in apple pie order.

On Tuesday the crew would drill with the boat, launching it in the surf and landing on the beach next to the station.

On Wednesday was signal drill: practice in sending and receiving messages using signal flags.

On Thursday the crew drilled using the rescue gear. The beach apparatus was set up, and practice run throughs were made with the breeches buoy.

On Friday the crew practiced resuscitation: the system of artificial respiration that revives people who have apparently drowned.

Saturday was wash day when the men washed their clothing and bedding and equipment.

[44]

Signalling with a flare

Sundays were free for church and religious observances.

A surfman had to be a citizen of the United States and not over 45 years of age. Every year he had to pass a thorough examination. If he were found to be anything other than completely fit for duty, he was discharged without pay or pension. To us today this seems highly unfair when we consider that most of the injuries these men got were received in the line of duty.

Captain

The captain, or station keeper, came up from the ranks of surfmen. He was responsible for all the property and equipment of the station. He had to be of good character, between 21 and 45 years old, and with enough schooling behind him to be able to handle the paper work that was part of his job. He had to fill out many reports, one for each wreck, and keep a daily journal. Not all the surfmen could handle a pencil as easily as they did an oar. These were days when some boys went to sea instead of to school. Though fearless and brave and wise to the ways of the world, some could not write much more than their own names.

On the first of August each year the crews would report at their stations and serve there for 10 months until June. In 1902, according to Dalton, the keepers were paid $900 per year, the surfmen $65 per month. The keeper remained on duty all year, even during the months of June and July when the ocean was least dangerous and storms least likely.

The surfmen were allowed one day a week to visit home between sunrise and sunset. Each took a turn at cooking meals for the others. The keeper, or captain, formed the station crew by numbers. The number 1 surfman was the most able, No. 2 the next, and so on down the line to the surfman newest to the ranks, and with the least experience. The surfmen wore their numerals on the upper arms of their dress uniform jackets.

Surfman

If the captain were absent, the No. 1 surfman took command of the station. Each surfman was given duty orders to follow and had to stand watches, or tours of duty, each day. Standing watches is a basic part of nautical life whether on ship or ashore.

Sharp lookouts were kept continually on the shore and horizon, day and night, for the entire ten-month duty season. Surfmen patrolled the beach night and day, no matter how severe a storm might be. This was almost always when the lifesaving service was needed the most.

On clear days the watch was kept from a lookout at the station or at some high rise from where the station's area of operation could be observed. In foggy or thick weather, the watch was by patrol at the water's edge. Every foot of beach was covered.

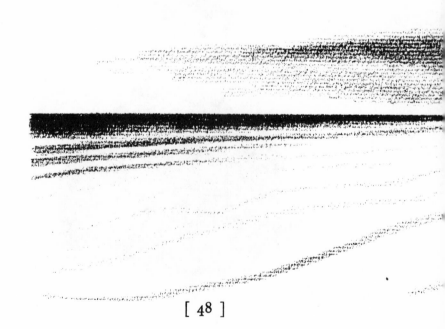

5 The Beach Patrol

Patrolling through the sand

The lifesaving stations were placed about five miles apart from each other. Each station patrolled 2½ miles on either side, meeting at a little hut or shelter called "the halfway house" between stations. Each night's patrol was made up of four watches: from sunset to 8 P.M., from 8 to 12, 12 to 4, and from 4 to sunrise. Two surfmen stood each watch.

The surfmen on patrol headed out from the station in opposite directions, staying as close to the surf as possible until they got to the halfway house. At the hut they were allowed to get in out of the weather and warm themselves. They also exchanged "checks." These were badge-shaped tokens on which the surfman's number and station were engraved.

If one of the surfmen on patrol did not arrive at the half-way house within a reasonable time, the other man on patrol walked in the direction of the other's station—along the other's "beat." In this manner the beach was always patrolled, and a second patrolman was quickly at the scene to lend a hand to the other, kept from checking in at the halfway house by an emergency situation found along his beat.

[51]

The surfman always carried a Coston signal flare with him. When he saw a vessel in danger he lit the flare. If the vessel had already struck, or run aground, the flare meant that help would soon be on its way to the crew. A flare was also lighted for vessels that were running too close to shore and were in danger of striking shoal or sandbar. The flare meant "Keep away—change course quickly!"

Surfman using Coston signal flare

6   Rescue by Breeches Buoy

On the way to safety

Brass projectile fired in Lyle gun

In Dalton's account of the lifesaving stations we read about the "apparatus," which was what the surfmen called the rescue gear they used. This was piled into a cart and rushed to the beach. Usually a horse was hitched to the cart. Often the horses would refuse to go forward in severe storms and had to be blindfolded.

Once at the scene the cart was quickly emptied. The mortar, called a Lyle-gun (in honor of its inventor Col. David A. Lyle of the United States Army) was loaded, then sighted and fired by the captain. It shot a long projectile, to which a line called the "shot-line" was attached. The captain always aimed for the rigging of the vessel in distress, keeping the shot well to windward. This way the line would be blown to the vessel even if it failed to land on the ship.

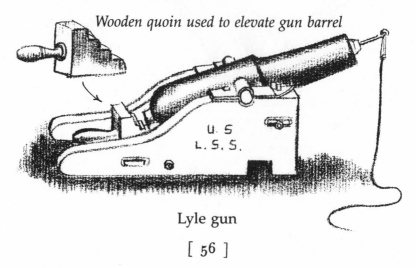

Wooden quoin used to elevate gun barrel

U. S
L. S. S.

Lyle gun

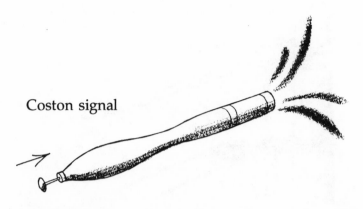

Coston signal

The lifesavers kept torches burning to let the stricken sailors know that a rescue attempt was being made. The sailors would then look for the shot line in the rigging. Often they would not be able to hear the firing of the Lyle-gun because of the fury of the storm. Most lifesaving captains were good marksmen with the gun, so the ship-wrecked crews knew that the burning torches meant a line had been fired and was usually on board somewhere.

They hauled in the shot line. Made fast to it was a tail block with a whip, an endless line, drawn through it. A piece of wood was attached to the block. Instructions were printed on it in English and French. The tail of the block was made fast to a mast. (See drawing.)

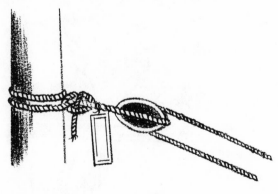

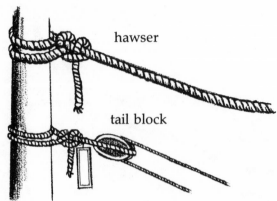

hawser

tail block

Then a stout 3-inch thick line (rope) called a hawser was bent (tied on) to the whip and hauled to the wreck by the surfmen. Sometimes they were helped by the stricken crews, but more often than not they had to do this themselves. The hawser was then attached to the mast of the wreck, about two feet above the tail block. (See drawing.)

When the hawser was fast to the mast, the surfmen tied their end of it to the strap of a sand anchor. Then they placed a bottom-heavy X-shaped wooden support called a crotch made of two 10-foot lengths of 2-inch x 3-inch wood, under the hawser and raised it. This pushed up against the hawser and made it taut, or tight. The survivors then came ashore on this line, often in the teeth of the howling storm.

sand anchor

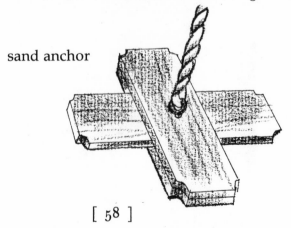

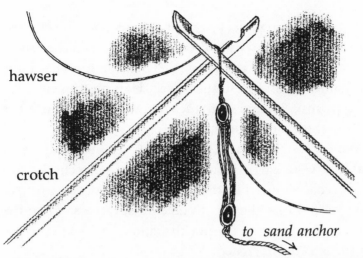

hawser

crotch

to sand anchor

The sand anchor was made of two 6-foot lengths of 2-inch x 8-inch hardwood crossed and bolted together at the center, where an iron ring was attached. A strap of rope on an iron hook ran from this ring to another called a "bull's eye." To this was attached a double pulley block that was then made fast to the end of the hawser. The sand anchor was buried in the sand. The hawser was pulled tighter still by the double pulley.

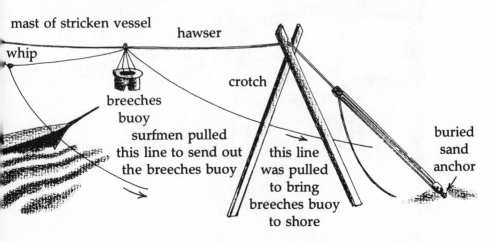

mast of stricken vessel

hawser

whip

breeches buoy
surfmen pulled this line to send out the breeches buoy

crotch

this line was pulled to bring breeches buoy to shore

buried sand anchor

A free-running block, called the traveler block, was then run onto the hawser. From it hung the breeches buoy, which was attached to the whip. Then the breeches buoy was hauled to and from the wreck. Hauling this line was often painful. Ice and sand stuck to it would rip the mittens and cut the hands of the surfmen.

Women and children were always rescued first. Small children were carried by someone, or tied securely into the breeches buoy. The captain and one of the surfmen always rushed into the surf to take off survivors. Then the breeches buoy would be quickly hauled back to the wreck for the next to be rescued.

The breeches buoy was made of an ordinary round ring-shaped cork life preserver. Attached to it were short canvas breeches. The rescued person sat in these breeches with the life ring around his waist, holding to the lengths of line that led to a ring fast to the traveler block. (See drawing.)

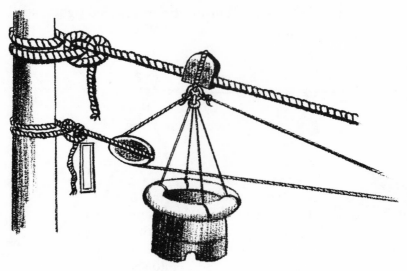

Breeches buoy ready for use

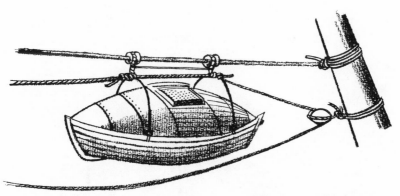

Life car ready for use

What was called a "life car" could be used instead of the breeches buoy, to rescue more people at one time. It looked like and was a small covered boat. Though it would hold more than the one person limit of the breeches buoy, it was not as easy to use. When a stricken vessel was about to break up quickly, the breeches buoy could be used on the hauling line alone, without taking the necessary time to rig the heavy hawser for the "life car." Since most of the shipping along the coasts was carried on in schooners and small vessels with crews of only six to ten men, this was another reason why the breeches buoy was used much more often than the life car.

The Lyle-gun had a range of almost 700 yards, but 200 yards was about the limit the shot-line method of rescue could be used. Beyond that, the wrecked crews could not haul the whip aboard against a strong current and anyone being hauled in by the breeches buoy had too far to travel. They could not stay alive exposed as they would be to the weather. Lifeboats were then used for rescue work.

7 Rescue by Lifeboat

Attempted rescue

Race Point surfboat

steering oar

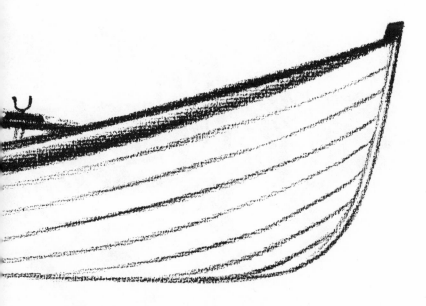

Along the seashore where the surf made launching a boat hard work, surfboats were the type of lifeboats used. The Monomoy and Race Point type surfboats used at the Cape Cod stations were 22 to 24 feet long. They were clinker-built of cedar, the lower edge of each plank overlapped the upper edge of the plank below it, and framed in white oak. Each end of the boat had an air chamber which made it buoyant. Along the sides of the boat were cork fenders which also helped keep it afloat and protected it from damage by the hull or wreckage from the stricken vessel.

Surfmen launching a surfboat

These surfboats were considered very light, though they weighed up to 1,000 pounds. They were preferred to the clumsier self-righting boat in use at other stations. The self-righting, or self-bailing boat, had watertight compartments and deck above the water line. It had what is called a freeing trunk or device which allowed water that came aboard to run out through the sides of the boat.

The surfboats were mounted on carts and drawn to the beach near the wreck. They were unloaded from the cart

and hauled into the surf. At just the right moment, they were run into the sea. The captain at his post at the stern was the last man to climb aboard. Surfmen whose posts were on shore waded up to their waists in the surf to help keep the boat upright.

As the men pulled at the oars, the captain steered from the stern with a long steering oar. He tried to keep away from the heavy, breaking waves and faced them head-on when nothing else could be done. As dangerous as this was, coming back to shore, or landing, was even worse.

The surfboat about to land was in peril from a "following" sea. It could not face a huge breaker, or comber, head-on. The undertow at the water's edge was powerful enough to pull a man to his death and smash up a boat. The crew would try to jump out of the boat as it neared the beach and run it up on the sand as quickly as possible, away from the undertow.

The captain of the surfboat had full command over those to be rescued. Even the captain of the vessel in distress had to obey his orders. This captain had to be the last to leave his ship to be sure all was in order before he left. Just as with the breeches buoy, women and children went first. No baggage was saved until all persons were rescued. If anyone brought his gear into the boat against the lifesaving captain's orders, it was thrown over the side.

Captain at steering oar commanding surfmen

Medicines were kept at the station to treat the injured and ill. Resuscitation or forms of artificial respiration were tried to save victims of drowning. Warm dry clothing was kept in ample supply, provided by the Women's National Relief Association. They collected articles of clothing and the needed funds to help victims of all sorts of disasters.

The saving of lives was only one part of the duty of the Lifesaving Service. It also saved millions of dollars worth of property. Ships that had run aground were often refloated. Cargo that had washed ashore was collected and protected from theft. It was covered and kept in good condition whenever possible. The Service also flashed warning signals to shipping in dangerous waters. And guarding the coast it helped prevent smugglers from landing with contraband.

REWARD OF MERIT

To
Isaac Hamblen,
for humane exertions in rescuing
the Captain and Crew of the
Sch.ʳ "Mary Anna",
on the outer Bar of
Nantucket Harbor,
Feb.ʸ 5.ᵗʰ 1871

COURAGE AND PERSEVERANCE

8

The medal for heroism of
The Massachusetts Humane Society.

The reverse of the medal cites a brave,
but in no way unusual, act of courage:
Hamblen and seven other Nantucketers
made their way across a thin crust
of ice on a bitter night to rescue
a freezing crew.

Seth Ellis

It is said much too often of days gone by that life was cheaper then. This is nonsense. The stories of the heroic men and women which follow are proof that the lives of complete strangers were as dear to them as their very own.

Time and again they went to the rescue of souls in distress at sea. It didn't matter to them what flag the stricken ship flew, what nationality or color the crew. Many lost their lives. Others were disabled for life, without hope of pension or aid. Irony played its part in the tragedies, too. Sometimes the panic and fear of those to be rescued resulted in the death of the rescuers. This happened in 1902 when almost the entire crew of the Monomoy Station perished trying to save five wrecked bargemen crazed with fear.

Seth Ellis was the only survivor of the Monomoy Life Saving Station crew. Here, in his own words, he tells the story of what happened:

"On Tuesday, March 11, 1902, about one o'clock A.M., the schooner barge *Wadena* stranded during a northeast gale and heavy sea on the Shovelful Shoal, off the southern end of Monomoy Island. The crew were rescued by our station crew. The barge remained on the shoal without showing any signs of going to pieces, and wreckers were engaged in lightering her cargo of coal. On the night of March 16 the weather became threatening, and all except five of the persons engaged in lightering the cargo were taken ashore from the barge by the tug *Peter Smith,* which was in the employ of the owners of the barge.

"Shortly before eight o'clock on the morning of March 17 one of the patrolmen from our station reported that the *Wadena* appeared to be in no immediate danger, but later Captain Eldredge received a message from Hyannis, inquiring whether everything was all right with the men aboard the barge. Up to this time no one at the station was aware that any persons had remained on the barge over night.

Barge *Wadena* in trouble

"Upon the receipt of this inquiry Captain Eldridge, putting on his hip boots and oil clothes, set out for the end of the Point, where he could personally ascertain the conditions.

"Arriving there he found that the barge was flying a signal of distress. He at once telephoned me, as I was the No. 1 man at the station, directing me to launch the surf-boat from the inside of the beach, and with the crew pull down to the Point. About two and one-half miles south of the station we took Captain Eldredge aboard and I gave him the steering oar.

"The wind was fresh from the southeast and there was a heavy sea running, but all the crew were of the opinion that the condition of the barge *Wadena* was not perilous, as she seemed to be sound and lying easy.

"Captain Eldredge decided to pull around the Point to the barge. At certain places on the shoals the sea was especially rough, and some water was shipped on the way out to the distressed craft, but without any trouble we succeeded in bringing our surf-boat under the lee of the barge just abaft the forerigging, the only place where it was practical to go alongside.

Lowering into boat

"As soon as we got alongside the barge a line was thrown aboard and quickly made fast by the persons on board. The persons on board the barge were all excited and wanted us to take them ashore as soon as we could. Captain Eldredge, without a moment's delay, when he found out the number of persons on board the barge and their desire to be taken ashore, directed them to get into the surf-boat.

"The seas were breaking heavily around the stern of the barge, and there was little room for operations in the smooth water, and the rail of the barge was twelve or thirteen feet above the surf-boat. Four of the five men lowered themselves over the side of the barge, one at a time, into the surf-boat, without mishap, by means of a rope, but the captain of the barge, who was a big, heavy man, let go his hold when part way down and dropped into the boat with such force as to break the after thwart. All five being safely in the boat, two were placed forward, two aft, and one amidships, and told to sit quietly and keep close down in the bottom of the boat.

"In order to get away from the barge quickly, the painter was cut, by orders of Captain Eldredge, and the surf-boat was at once shoved off. In order to clear the line of breakers that extended from the stern of the barge so that we could lay a good course for the shore, a part of the surfmen were backing hard on the port oars, while the others gave way with full power on the starboard side. Before we could get the boat turned around a big wave struck us with fearful force, and quite a lot of water poured into the surf-boat.

"Captain Eldredge stood in the stern of the boat with the steering oar in his hand giving his orders, and the surfmen stuck to their posts.

"As soon as the water came into the boat, the rescued men jumped up, and becoming panic-stricken, threw their arms about the necks of the surfmen so that none of us could use our oars. The seas, one after another, struck us, and the boat, filling with water, turned bottom up, throwing us all into the raging sea. The seas kept striking us after the boat upset, and we were soon in among the heaviest breakers. Twice we righted the boat, but the seas which

Panic in a boat

struck her before we could get into her capsized her each time.

"After righting the boat twice, our strength was fast leaving us, and we all knew that we could not survive long without assistance. The five men that we had taken off the barge were the first to be swept off the overturned boat and to perish before our eyes. They did not regain a hold of the boat after she turned over the first time, and were quickly swept to death.

"All of us clung to the boat, giving each other all the encouragement that we could. Surfman Chase was the first one of our crew to perish, then Nickerson and Small were swept to death. Captain Eldredge, Surfmen Kendrick, Foye and Rogers and myself still managed to hold to the boat. Every sea which struck the boat swept completely over us, almost smothering us. Kendrick was the next one of our crew to perish, and poor Foye soon followed him. Captain Eldredge and Surfman Rogers and myself were the only ones left, and we expected that we, too, would soon share the fate of our comrades.

"Rogers was clinging to the boat about amidships, while Captain Eldredge and myself were holding on near the stern. Captain Eldredge called to me to help him to get a better hold, and I managed to pull him on to the bottom of the boat, when a sea struck us and washed us both off. I managed to regain a hold on the bottom of the boat, and looking around for Captain Eldredge, I saw that he was holding on to the spar and sail which had drifted from underneath the boat, but was still fast to it. The seas were washing me off the boat continually at this time, and when I last saw our brave captain, he was drifting away from the boat, holding on to the spar and sail.

"My strength was fast going, and when poor Rogers begged me to help him climb further up onto the boat, the only thing I could do was to tell him that we were drifting towards the beach, and that help would soon be at hand and to hold on.

"Rogers had lost his strength, however, and failing to get a more secure place on the bottom of the boat, feebly moaning, 'I have got to go,' he fell off the boat and sank beneath the waters.

"I was now alone on the bottom of the boat, and seeing that the center board had slipped part way out, I managed to get hold of it, and holding it with one hand succeeded in getting my oil clothes, undercoat, vest, and boots off.

Hanging on for dear life

"By that time the overturned boat had drifted down over the shoals in the direction of the barge *Fitzpatrick*, which was also stranded on the shoals, and when I sighted the craft I waved my hand as a signal for help. I soon saw those on the barge fling a dory over the side into the water, but could see nothing more of the dory after that on account of the mist and high sea until it hove in sight with a man in it rowing towards me. The man in the dory was brave Capt. Elmer F. Mayo. He ran the dory alongside of me, and with his help I got into the boat. I was so used up that I was speechless, and all that I could do was to kneel in the bottom of the boat and hold on to the thwarts. To land in the dory through the surf was a perilous undertaking, but Mayo, who is a skilled boatman, carefully picked his way over the rips and headed his little boat for the shore.

"Surfman Bloomer of our station, who had been left ashore, had walked down to the Point to assist Captain Eldredge and crew in landing, and when he saw Mayo fighting his way through the breakers, he ran down into the surf, seized the little boat, and helped Mayo to land safely.

"Bloomer was told of the terrible tragedy by Captain Mayo, as I was unable to speak at the time. As I have often said, 'If the persons we took off the barge had kept quiet as we told them to, all hands would have been landed in safety.'"

Elmer F. Mayo

Captain Elmer F. Mayo was known ever after as "The Hero of Monomoy." He was born on Cape Cod at Chatham and was an expert and fearless boat handler. Except for a brief try at prospecting for gold in the Klondike, during the great Klondike Gold Rush of 1896-1899, he worked as a boatman and fisherman. He also dragged for anchors that were lost and worked as a wrecker, taking off whatever could be salvaged from stranded vessels and helping to re-float ones that could be saved.

On that fateful day in March 1902, Captain Mayo was on board the barge *Fitzpatrick* with a Captain Mallows, also of Chatham, and another man, the captain of the barge. The *Fitzpatrick* had run aground at about the same time as the *Wadena*. All remained on board the barge overnight to be ready for a full day's work of refloating it at the first light of dawn.

The wind picked up at night and Captain Mayo hauled aboard a small dory in case they should need it to get ashore. There were no oars for the dory so he cut down a large pair he found and made makeshift thole pins for them, as there were no oarlocks either.

Capt. Mayo in his dory

Soon the wind was blowing a gale, and rough water was churning all around the barges. A thick fog settled in the morning that kept those aboard the *Fitzpatrick* from seeing the *Wadena*. A distress signal was flying from the rigging of the *Wadena*.

The first shock came to Mayo and Mallows when they saw the station's overturned lifeboat floating by, with Surfman Ellis clinging to it. They knew then that a terrible disaster had taken place. Mayo stripped off his heavy outer clothes and dashed for the dory. Captain Mallows begged him not to go for fear he, too, would be drowned.

Paying Mallows no heed, he flung the dory into the pounding sea and slid down a rope to it. He was clad only in his underwear. The cut-down oars were so thick that he could hardly get a grip on them. The sea was raging and the March gale cold and driving. Yet he endured, struggling against what was almost the impossible. It would have been—for anyone else but Mayo.

By sheer personal courage and determination he kept the overturned life-boat in sight and finally got within calling distance. He told Ellis to hang on, that he would reach him. And so he did. What is more, in the chop and gale, he got Ellis off the lifeboat and into the dory with him. This could not have been done except for the fact that they were both experienced in the skill of boat rescue.

Trying to land in heavy surf

To land the little dory through the surf was another impossible task—for anyone else. But Mayo knew how. Cool and calm, he picked his way in the fog through the shoals and rips to a point where he could land with some hope of their both getting ashore alive. Surfman Bloomer, of the Monomoy station saw the dory and came running to it. He was able to dash into the surf and help drag the dory ashore.

Captain Mayo was presented with medals by the United States government and the Massachusetts Humane Society.

It is hard to imagine that anyone could ever live long enough to make a career out of saving lives at sea, but several hardy souls did, one of them a woman! She was the famous Ida Lewis, of Newport, Rhode Island. Ida was born in 1842, the daughter of Captain Hosea Lewis, the lighthouse keeper of Lime Rock Light. At sixteen, she had already saved four boys from drowning when they overturned their sailboat. By 1869 she had saved eleven persons and was awarded a silver medal and $100 from the Life Saving Benevolent Society of New York. Edward Rowe Snow, in his excellent book "Famous Lighthouses of New England," tells us that pictures of Ida appeared in the most popular American magazines of the day. She was a national hero.

Mr. Snow tells us that in the same year, on the Fourth of July, the residents of Newport presented her with a new lifeboat, which she rowed away to Lime Rock Light while the assembled crowd cheered. The President of the United States, General Ulysses S. Grant, and the Vice-President, Schuyler Colfax, also visited this heroic girl in the same year. Mr. Snow relates that President Grant, hero of the Civil War, was fascinated by the stories Miss Lewis told him of her life at the light. General William T. Sherman and Admiral George Dewey also came to Lime Rock Light to meet Ida Lewis.

Ida Lewis, at 64, made her twenty-third rescue. By 1907, at the age of 66, she had been at Lime Rock Light, on duty, for fifty years! This is the remarkable story of a courageous woman, appointed keeper at Lime Rock Light by a special act of Congress.

Opposite: Ida Lewis, as a national hero,
on the cover of *Harper's Weekly* for July 31, 1869

HARPER'S WEEKLY.

JOURNAL OF CIVILIZATION.

VOL. XIII.—No. 657.]   NEW YORK, SATURDAY, JULY 31, 1869.   [SINGLE COPIES, TEN CENTS. $4.00 PER YEAR IN ADVANCE.

Entered according to Act of Congress, in the Year 1869, by Harper & Brothers, in the Clerk's Office of the District Court of the United States, for the Southern District of New York.

MISS IDA LEWIS, THE HEROINE OF NEWPORT.—Phot. by Manchester Brothers, Providence, R. I.—[See Page 484.]

Like Ida Lewis, many brave souls went to the aid of others not as members of the Humane Society of the Government Lifesaving Service, but as private citizens going gallantly to the rescue of those in need.

In 1842 the British ship *Josephus* was wrecked on the Peaked Hill Bars at the tip of Cape Cod. Two young men of Truro named Daniel Cassidy and Jonathan Collins went to rescue the ill-fated crew in a dory. But the heavy seas were too much for the frail small boat and both men were lost before they could reach the ship.

Others, such as Isaac Norton of Vineyard Haven, on Martha's Vineyard, were luckier. In the great Portland Storm of 1898 the harbor of Vineyard Haven was strewn with wreckage. Only a few lives were lost, however, thanks to the courage and skill of Captain "Ike" Norton. In a borrowed dory, with Alvin H. Cleveland, Frank Golart and Stanley Fisher, he saved five men from the schooner *Hamilton*. Back out in the storm again he, Cleveland and F. Horton Johnson saved another five men—this time from the schooner *Thurlow*. Once more Norton went out. The storm was at its height and those on shore strongly urged him not to go. But he did; and with the help of Cleveland and Golart brought back five more victims who owed their lives to these men of great courage.

Heading for shore

James Lopes

James Lopes of Provincetown was a brave fisherman who risked his life in the same storm. As a member of a volunteer crew, he helped rescue a stricken crew from a wreck in Provincetown Harbor. He received a medal for his heroism and a job with a government lifesaving crew. He became No. 5 surfman of the Cahoon's Hollow Station, Wellfleet.

Daniel Cole

Captain Daniel Cole, keeper of the Cahoon's Hollow station had been a member since the service began on Cape Cod. He went to sea at nine to fish the Grand Banks; in his early teens he plied the Great Lakes in the Midwest as a trader. At the age of nineteen he joined the United States Army, fought with an Illinois regiment and marched through Georgia with General Sherman. He went back to

Breeches buoy in operation

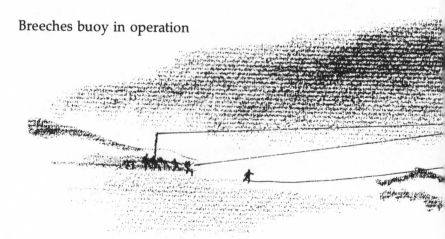

Grand Banks fishing after the war, serving with the life-saving service as a surfman when the fishing season was over.

On New Year's eve, 1890, he and his crew saved fifteen men from the crew of the schooner *Smuggler* which was dashed to pieces in the freezing night. The fury of the storm was so great that the surfmen were blinded. Great gusts of wind hurled sand in their eyes. Their faces stung from the force of it. Even the station horse halted, unable to pull the equipment further. After a heroic struggle, the men reached the beach opposite the wreck. A shot was fired over it and made fast. The schooner was breaking up quickly. But the breeches buoy was rigged and the crew pulled safely ashore, though half-dead from the cold. No sooner was the last man landed than the *Smuggler* disappeared from sight, smashed to bits in the heavy surf.

Capt. James's Landing, Hull, in the 1880s

Among the early lifesavers, a man of great courage and compassion was William Tewksbury. In 1817 he and his son, in their sailing canoe, saved seven people from drowning off Deer Island, Winthrop. This was done at great risk; the extra weight of the rescued in a small canoe was very dangerous. Tewksbury, however, was not one to let such things stand in his way. Edward Rowe Snow writes in his book, *The Romance of Boston Bay*, that Tewksbury was awarded a medal for this act by the Massachusetts Humane Society and that, by the year 1825, the Tewksbury family had saved thirty-one lives.

Without question the greatest lifesaving family of all was the James family of Hull, Massachusetts. William James came to America from the Netherlands where his name was spelled Jaames. He was the assistant to Moses B. Tower, the first lifesaver of the Massachusetts Humane Society at Hull. Tower was a fearless and skillful rescuer but had to make his living as a hotel manager—there were no salaries for lifesavers in those days.

Figurehead of the *Maritana*

William James took part in many rescues, including that of the crew of the brig *Tremont,* wrecked at Point Allerton, near Hull, in 1844. William James also owned a dozen schooners that carried cobblestones to Boston, used to pave the streets in those days. It is said that he gave one of the vessels to each of his sons when they reached manhood.

One of his sons, Samuel, designed a good, seaworthy life-boat. He was also a daring lifesaver. In 1861 he was awarded a certificate and $10 from the Massachusetts Humane Society for the rescue of twelve persons from the ship *Maritana* wrecked near Boston Light. Captain Samuel James made many trips in a small boat through the early November gale and rainstorm to pick up survivors from the wreckage of the *Maritana.*

Young Joshua James sighting his
brother's schooner, *Hepzibah*

The most famous member of the James family, and cer-
tainly the most famous lifesaver of all time, was Samuel's
brother, Joshua. Joshua was only ten years old when he
made up his mind to dedicate his life to saving others.

The day was the third of April in 1837. He was standing
on a hill in Hull waiting to catch a glimpse of his brother
Reiner's schooner *Hepzibah*. Joshua's mother and baby
sister were on board. When the schooner was off Hull Gut
a fierce squall blew in. Joshua saw the wind wreak havoc
with the *Hepzibah*. When the vessel capsized he ran home
with the terrible news. Joshua's mother and the baby were
lost.

Joshua James

Not much else is known about Joshua's early years. He went to sea and in due time he was known to be a first-rate pilot. It was said that he had a magic sense of seeing through the mist and fog—that he always knew where he was. "I can hear the land talk to me," was his simple explanation.

He was only fifteen when he took part in his first rescue with the Massachusetts Humane Society. By 1850 he was awarded a medal for heroism. On April 1 of that year he helped rescue the crew of the French brig *L'Essai* lost at Nantasket Beach. Seven years later he was honored for his bravery in the rescue of the crew of the ship *Delaware,* wrecked on Toddy Rocks. In 1876 he was made keeper of four Humane Society stations—at Stony Beach and Point Allerton, and two at Nantasket Beach. In 1885 he and his crew saved all the crew of the brig *Anita Owen,* which struck in a storm on Nantasket Beach. The next year, the Humane Society presented him with a large silver medal that read:

"To Captain Joshua James for brave and faithful service of more than 40 years in the lifeboats of the Humane Society 1886."

Three years later the Society presented him with its highest award, its gold medal, for saving twenty-eight lives from four vessels in the great storm of November 25-26, 1888. The United States government also awarded gold medals to Captain James and ten of his crew.

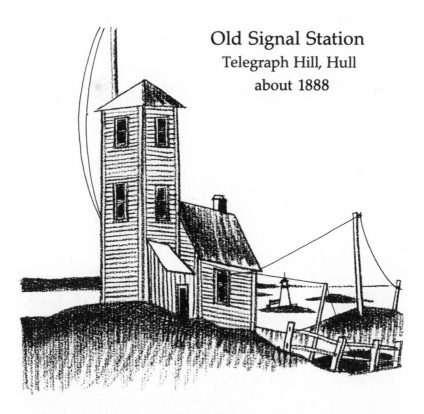

Old Signal Station
Telegraph Hill, Hull
about 1888

The November Storm of 1888 was one of the worst of the nineteenth century. Along eight miles of beach where James had posts, five helpless vessels were smashed. A violent northeast gale brought with it a blinding snow-storm and huge high tides. Early on the morning of No-vember 25, Captain James and some hardy crew members clawed their way to the top of Telegraph Hill, in Hull. Now and again they could see through the snow and spot ships trying to ride out the howling storm. By early after-noon Captain James had ordered out the beach patrol. What follows is a detailed account of Joshua James's next twenty-four hours, from the Annual Report of the United States Life Saving Service, 1889.

"In the afternoon of the 25th [November 1888] the veteran life-saver Captain Joshua James, of Hull, observing several vessels dragging their anchors in Nantasket Roads, called together a crew of sturdy fishermen and got the [Massachusetts Humane] society's surf-boat the *R. B. Forbes*, ready for use. No sooner had this been done than a large schooner stranded a short distance west of Toddy Rocks, but the sea was so high that it was thought best to fire a line to her and land the crew by means of the breeches-buoy. With the assistance of a number of residents of the neighborhood this task was successfully accomplished. Meanwhile the coal-laden schooner *Gertrude Abbott* of Philadelphia, Pennsylvania, struck the rocks about an eighth of a mile to the eastward and hoisted a signal of distress in the rigging. She was so far off that it was at once apparent that communication could not be effected without the beach-apparatus. It was now growing dark, the tide was high, and the storm was raging with increased fury. These conditions prompted James and his men to

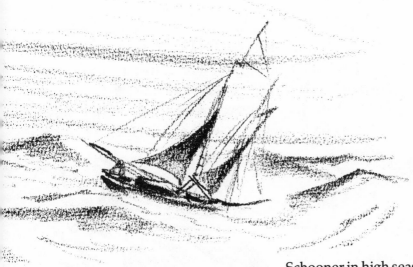

Schooner in high seas

wait for lower water before attempting a launch. A fire was set ablaze on a bluff so that the vessel could be kept in view. The tide fell but little, owing to the violence of the gale, and between 8 and 9 o'clock at night the men decided not to delay longer, but to undertake to board the schooner. They managed to launch the surf-boat through the furious breakers and bent vigorously to the oars. Two of the crew were obliged to bail constantly to keep the boat from swamping. The vessel was lying head-to, and the volunteers, after a desperate pull got near enough to heave a line on the bow. The eight sailors then swung themselves by means of a rope into the boat and a start was made for the beach. The wind and sea were sweeping wildly along the shore, which made the return exceedingly hazardous; besides, the boat, being crowded, with little or no room to work the oars, was hard to manage. When within two hundred yards of the beach it struck a rock, filled, and rolled one side deep under. The occupants quickly shifted to windward and succeeded in righting the boat, although one man fell overboard, but fortunately was hauled in by his comrades before the sea could sweep him beyond reach. Captain James admonished everyone to stick to the boat as long as possible. It struck the rocks a number of times and was buffeted along at the mercy of the waves, the men just managing with the few oars that were left to keep it headed

On the rocks

for the shore so that the sea might heave it in. It is a wonder that it was not completely capsized in the breakers or demolished amongst the ledges. Finally it was thrown upon the rocks in shoal water and all hands promptly jumped out and scrambled safely ashore. The schooner's crew were immediately taken to a neighboring house and comfortably cared for. This was a notable rescue and one that put to the test the noble qualities of every member of the boat's crew. Actuated by the highest motives, they set forth amidst untold peril and triumphed by their cool courage and determination of purpose. There are few examples of greater heroism. During the remainder of the night a strict watch was kept along the beach, and at 3 o'clock in the morning of the 26th Captain James was again called out. The wind was blowing with unusual violence, accompanied by rain and sleet.

"At daybreak James had assembled another boat's crew, composed in part of those who had gone with him to the *Gertrude Abbott,* and they pulled out the sunken schooner *Bertha F. Walker* and took from the rigging seven men who were in danger of perishing.

"In the latter part of the forenoon Captain James and his men were summoned to the assistance of the schooner *H. C. Higginson,* ashore on Nantasket Beach. . . . When it became evident that the efforts of the volunteer forces to bring off the sailors by means of the breeches-buoy would fail, Captain James and his men launched the large surf-boat, the *Nantasket,* which had been brought to the scene. The sea was very rough and breaking heavily along side the stranded vessel. After a hard pull the boat was rowed near enough to the schooner, which was lying stern to the shore, so that the men could throw a line on board.

"A sailor who was in the mizzen rigging then came cautiously down the shrouds and tying the line around his body leaped overboard and was hauled into the boat. The latter by dint of hard work on the part of the oarsmen was then forced forward abreast of the mainmast. The rest of the sailors, four in number, were in the fore rigging and

Attempting a rescue

very much exhausted from their long exposure. It was with the greatest difficulty that they walked their way, by aid of the hawser which had previously been sent to them, to the main rigging; then fastening lines to themselves they in turn jumped into the breakers and were hauled one by one into the surf-boat and taken safely to the shore amid the enthusiastic cheers of many spectators who were anxiously watching the proceedings from the beach. The half-starved and half-frozen men were quickly conveyed in carriages to the home of Selectman David O. Wade, of Hull, where they were rubbed dry, warmed, and furnished with a change of clothing. Three of the schooner's crew lost their lives at this wreck. The captain and one other were washed overboard in the night and a third died in the rigging from exposure.

"The Humane Society's men by their zealous and answering work rescued some twenty-eight people from different vessels in distress during this great storm. When it is considered that they imperiled their lives practically without hope of reward, influenced solely by the desire to succor their fellow-creatures, too much praise cannot be accorded them. Gold medals were awarded to Captain James and the following men who composed his crew at the rescue of those on board the *Gertrude Abbott:* G. F. Pope, L. F. Galiano, A. B. Mitchell, Joseph Galiano, O. F. James, A. L. Mitchell, E. T. Pope, J. L. Mitchell, Frederick Smith, and H. W. Mitchell. Upon those who did not participate in that rescue, but who with some of those already mentioned made up the boat's crew that went to the *H. C. Higginson,* silver medals were conferred. These were Eugene Mitchell, Alfred Galiano, George Augustus, Eugene Mitchell, Jr., and W. B. Mitchell."

In imminent danger

Other lifesaving stations played a part in these same rescue operations. But their efforts could not compare with the almost superhuman and overwhelming role of Joshua James.

Captain James remained in service all of his life.

When the United States government established a lifesaving station nearby at Stoney Beach, Captain James was the obvious choice to be keeper. But he was already 62 years old and the age limit was 45! The lifesaving service made his case a special one—the only time it ever did so while it was in operation—and James was given the post. Then he was made keeper of the Point Allerton Station where he served until his death at 75 in 1902.

In 1901 he still was fit enough to pass a physical examination required of all men on duty. The loss of the members of the lifesaving crew at the Monomoy disaster the following year is said to have brought him great sorrow. Within days he was dead. Even in his sixty-first year of service he handled the long heavy steering oar, putting his crew through rugged boat drills. One morning when they came ashore, Joshua leaped gracefully out of the boat, as he had done thousands of times. He noticed the ebb of the tide and remarked on it. Even as he did, the tide of his own life ran out. The next moment he was dead, lying face down on the wet beach. There was no rescue that could be made for him. His gallant heart had finally stopped, after so many heroic years.

Surfman signalling with flare

Joshua James was one of the many people who risked their lives as a matter of course to save others.

When the fury of a storm was at its highest, and most of their neighbors were at home, snug and dry, the surfmen went out; their work was just beginning. As long as the storm raged they stayed at their posts, without food or rest, until the rescue work was finished.

Heavy surf

Take a walk along the shore on a foul, disagreeable day. If a blustery northeaster makes the going difficult, so much the better. Pick out a spot a mile or more from shore and imagine that in this spot a vessel is breaking apart. On this vessel are a dozen strangers from just about anywhere in the world and they are about to drown. You do not have to hear their shouts or be able to understand their language to know that they are begging you to save them.

Imagine that the time of year is January and the temperature is at zero. Imagine, too, that it is night. Then think about these men: Sam Fisher, Joshua James, and all the others. Consider these men, and what they did.

Old light at Minot's Ledge in Boston Harbor
knocked down by waves in the great storm
of April 17, 1851.

Appendix

Glossary

A square-rigger in trouble off Cape Cod

Barge—A large boat used for carrying goods. The barges mentioned in this book had no power and were pulled along by towboats, or tugboats.

Boat Carriage—The surfboats were secured to a high-wheeled rig much in the way boats are carried on boat trailers today. The boat carriage was pulled by the surfmen or by horses kept at the station for that purpose.

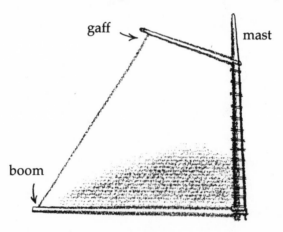

Boom—A spar, or pole used to extend the bottom of a sail.

Breeches Buoy—Short canvas breeches attached to an ordinary round ring life preserver. ·

BRIG

Brig—A two-masted, square-rigged vessel.

[108]

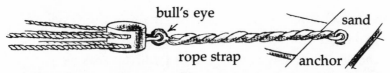

bull's eye   sand

rope strap   anchor

BULL'S EYE—The iron ring attached to the strap that was itself attached to the sand anchor.

CANVAS—Sails were made of canvas and spoken of as canvas.

CAPSIZE—To upset or overturn a vessel.

cork fender

planked sides

CLINKER-BUILT—A boat with planked sides. The lower edge of each plank overlaps the upper edge of the plank beneath it like clapboards on a house.

CORK FENDERS—A protective padding of cork that was attached to the gunwales of the surfboats. It protected the sides of the boats from damage and helped to make the boats buoyant.

COSTON SIGNAL—The brilliant red flare carried by the surfmen, used for signaling at night.

CROTCH—The tent-shaped device made of 2 ten-foot lengths of 2 in. x 3 in. wood fastened together at the top and used to support the hawser. See drawing.

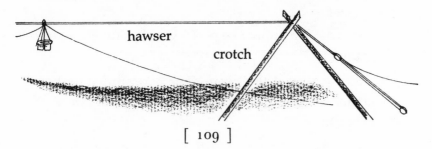

hawser

crotch

DISTRESS SIGNAL—An S.O.S. signifying that the vessel was in danger of sinking. Often it was accomplished by flying the vessel's flag upside down, or by firing rockets.

DORY—A small flat-bottomed rowboat with a sharp prow and flaring sides.

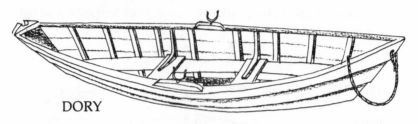

DORY

DRAG—This was a canvas bucket attached to a line and flung overboard. It acted as a brake and retarded the progress of a boat that was being swept along by the wind.

FAKING BOX—A wooden box in which the shot line was coiled in layers on wooden pins. When the pins were taken out the line is free to be paid out without snarling or entanglement.

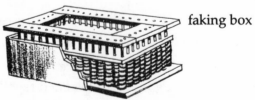

faking box

FOLLOWING SEA—Waves that follow, or come up behind a vessel.

GUNWALE—The upper edge of a vessel's side. Pronounced "gunnel."

HAWSER—A large, thick rope. The hawser used in the life-saving apparatus supported the breeches buoy. (See Whip.)

heaving stick   heaving line

HEAVING LINE—A small line that was attached to a heaving stick. The stick could be thrown about fifty yards to a vessel or bit of wreckage where the line was then attached.

KEEPER—The station keeper of the lifesaving station. Keepers in government service held the rank of captain in the United States Life Saving Service.

LEEWARD—The side away from the wind. The lee side of a vessel is out of the wind. See drawing.

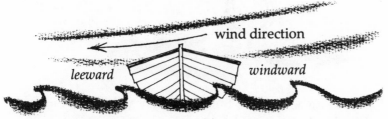

wind direction

leeward   *windward*

LIFEBOAT—A boat used to rescue the shipwrecked. Self-righting and self-bailing lifeboats were used where they could be launched down ways or ramps into the sea. Many were fitted with motors. Lighter weight boats, called surfboats, were also used.

LIFE CAR—A boat of ribbed metal which could be fastened to the hawser. It had a closed cover and could carry several passengers at one time.

LIFE JACKET—A cloth vest in which pieces of cork were sewn for buoyancy.

LYLE GUN—A small bronze cannon named for its inventor, Col. David A. Lyle of the United States Army. The Lyle gun fired an 18-pound iron projectile to which a line, called the shot line, was attached.

[111]

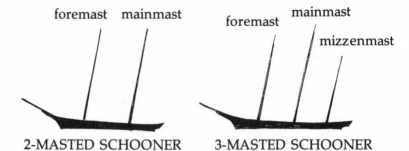

foremast   mainmast

foremast   mainmast   mizzenmast

2-MASTED SCHOONER   3-MASTED SCHOONER

MAINMAST, MIZZENMAST—See drawing.

OARLOCK—A fitting at the gunwale of a boat which holds the oar in place.

oarlock

PATROLMAN'S CLOCK—Similar to a watchman's clock, it could only be wound with a special key.

PILOT—A person licensed to take a vessel in and out of port.

PORT—The left side of a vessel.

RIGGING—The ropes and chains used to stay the masts, support the spars, and trim (control) the sails of a vessel.

SAILING CANOE—A canoe to which a mast and sail have been added.

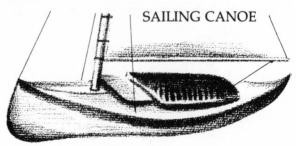

SAILING CANOE

SAND ANCHOR—Two six-foot lengths of 2 in. x 8 in. hardwood crossed and bolted together at the center and buried in the sand. (See Whip.)

SCHOONER—A vessel with two or more masts and a fore-and-aft rig.

SCHOONER

SELF-BAILING—A boat with a freeing trunk or device that allows water to run out through the sides.

SELF-RIGHTING—A boat that will float to the surface and right itself automatically.

SHOT LINE—The line carried by the shot fired from the mortar or Lyle gun.

SLATTING—Violent slapping, beating of sails or spars being whipped about by the wind.

SLOOP—A small vessel with one mast and a fore-and-aft rig. See drawing.

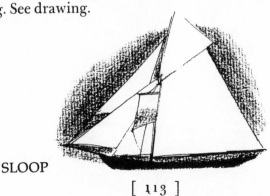

SLOOP

SPAR—The name for any round timber such as a mast, boom, gaff, or yard, used aboard ship.

SQUALL—A sudden and violent gust of wind often accompanied by rain or snow.

STARBOARD—The right side of a vessel.

FORE

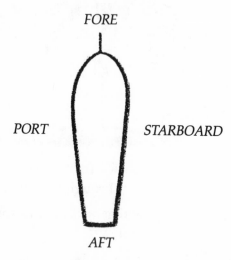

PORT   STARBOARD

AFT

SURF—The swell of the ocean, or the waves breaking on shore.

SURFBOAT—The lighter type of boat used by lifesavers. It was light enough to be taken off its carriage or cart, and run into the sea, carried by the surfmen.

hawser

SURFMEN—The enlisted men of the lifesaving service.

SWAMPING—Filling with water and capsizing or sinking.

TAIL BLOCK—This was attached to the shot line. The whip was drawn through it. The tail block was made fast to a mast aboard a stricken vessel. (See Whip.)

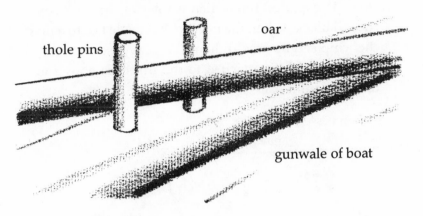

THOLE PINS—Pegs set in the gunwale of a boat which served as a fulcrum or pivot for the oars.

TRAVELER BLOCK—This was a free running block or pulley that ran on the hawser. The breeches buoy hung from it.

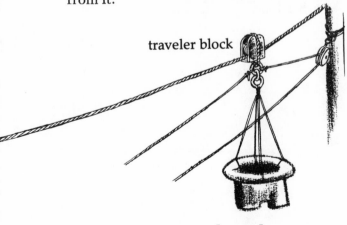

UNDERTOW—The strong current that runs out to sea along the bottom where there is heavy surf and breaking waves.

WINDWARD—The side facing the point from which the wind blows. (See Leeward.)

WHIP—The endless line which is rove, or drawn through the tail block. When the tail block is made fast to a mast, the whip can be used to haul the heavy hawser aboard. Then the whip is attached to the breeches buoy and is used to haul it back and forth.

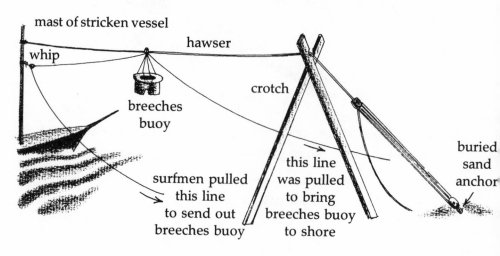

THE PAST IN PERSPECTIVE
Heroes of Peace, 1898

The following pages contain an article devoted to accounts of heroism by individual members of the U.S. Life Saving Service.

The article appeared in *The Century* magazine, which— with *Harper's* and *Scribner's*— was one of the most influential and respected monthly magazines published in this country.

In 1898 *The Century* began a series of articles entitled "Heroes of Peace." Gustav Kobbé wrote about acts of heroism in the lighthouse service, and the lifesaving service. His story of the lifesaving service is reproduced in its entirety.

Other series authors included Theodore Roosevelt, on heroism and bravery of the police; and Jacob Riis, heroic deeds of firefighters.

—P.G.

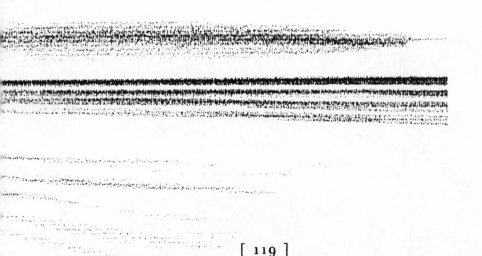

Heroes of the Life Saving Service

by Gustav Kobbé

from *The Century Magazine* of April 1898.

Illustration from an original etching,
"The Life Line" by Winslow Homer,
which accompanied the article.

THERE is one power that wages a ceaseless war against whomsoever ventures upon its domain—the sea. No enemy is more pitiless. Wind and snow and fog are its weapons. It neither asks nor gives quarter. Who shall say how many centuries man has sailed the main? But, also, who shall say how many ships and how many lives it has claimed as tribute? With a kind of savage sarcasm, it often calls in its very ópposite, the land, to aid in its work of destruction, so that what should be the sailors' hope and haven becomes at times his source of greatest peril.

A few nations, having awakened to a sense of their responsibility toward humanity, have sought to lessen this last and most cruel peril, so far as lies in human power, and maintain each a little band of men whose duty it is to patrol the coast, watch out for stranded vessels, and go to the rescue of their crews.

In the United States these men belong to what is known as the Life-saving Service. Year after year they are called upon to brave dangers before which the stoutest heart might well quail, and brave them calmly and coolly, without the stimulus of excitement which in battle carries everything along, and often makes a fictitious hero of a natural coward.

There is nothing fictitious in the heroism of the life-savers. They are aware of the possible consequences of their every act. Desperate chances are taken, but they are known to be desperate. As a plain recital of some of the rescues they have made will show, they deliberately go forth to save the lives of others, knowing they are imperiling their own; and this, too, without the hope of any adequate reward in case they are successful. There can be no truer « heroes of peace » than they.

For administrative purposes, the sea-coast and lake shores of the United States have been divided into twelve districts, each with a superintendent of life-saving stations. These superintendents, though supposed merely to exercise a general oversight, are often summoned at critical moments, and

personally assist in the work of rescue. Of their small number, two have been drowned, one has escaped that fate by the merest chance, and another has died of exposure.

Another district superintendent, Jerome G. Kiah, with headquarters at Sand Beach, Michigan, is one of the heroes of the Life-saving Service. He holds the gold medal, the highest award the United States government can bestow for heroism in saving life. His name is associated with what was both one of the most daring attempts at rescue and one of the greatest tragedies of the service —a tragedy which wiped out an entire crew, with the exception of this sole survivor.

Mr. Kiah was at the time keeper of the Point aux Barques life-saving station on Lake Huron. A vessel struck too far out to be reached with the shot and line. The peril of attempting a rescue with the surfboat was only too apparent; but Keeper Kiah mustered his men, and made the launch. For a while their strength and skill enabled them to surmount or push through the tumultuous seas; but, once in the open lake beyond the shoals, where the storm was free to riot at will, the real danger began. It was a test beyond human powers. The keeper remembers that twice the boat capsized and was righted. After that he has a vague recollection of the boat capsizing and righting herself several times, and of the crew clinging to it until, one by one, the surfmen, perishing of cold, let go their hold, and vanished beneath the waves. He has a dim remembrance of the boat, with himself clinging to it, grating over the shoal, and then being flung up on shore.

He was found by two men, standing, with one hand on the root of a fallen tree, steadying himself with a lath in the other, and swaying as if walking, but not stirring his feet—a dazed, tottering wreck of his former self, murmuring in an incoherent way:

« Poor boys! Poor boys! They are all gone —all gone!» Temporarily shattered in mind and body, he was obliged to resign from the service. He was long in recovering, but finally it was possible practically to reward his bravery with the appointment to his present position.

Keeper Silas H. Harding and his crew of the Jerry's Point, New Hampshire, station all received gold medals for a rescue the perils of which were almost unique. During a winter storm, with the thermometer below freezing-point, the schooner *Oliver Dyer* stranded on the ledges, a hundred and fifty yards from shore. As the life-savers were about to fire a life-line from the Lyle gun, a heavy sea caught the vessel on her broadside, and, lifting her bodily, threw her thirty or forty feet inshore, where the wash was so great that it would have been impossible to handle the line. The vessel now gradually worked shoreward to within about seventy-five feet of a large, flat, ice-covered, wave-swept rock.

Keeper Harding at once realized that it was from this rock the battle must be fought.

He and his crew succeeded in reaching it between seas. They had barely gained a footing when they saw a man struggling in the breakers. Surfman Hall sprang to his rescue, but as he dragged him out, a wave swept both off the rock. Fortunately, they were carried to the inshore side, and, clinging to its ragged edges, his hands and arms torn and bleeding, the surfman was able, as the sea receded a moment, to regain his footing and draw the sailor up after him. Meanwhile, Surfman Randall had saved another man just as he was being carried out a second time by the undertow. Keeper Harding now made a successful throw with the heaving-stick; and as the men leaped from the vessel, with the line under the armpits, they were hauled ashore, whither the life-savers had retreated after they had succeeded in throwing the line to the vessel.

In their exhausted state no information could be obtained from the men who were rescued as to the number that were aboard the wreck; and Keeper Harding, fearing, although no more signals for help came over the line, that there still might be sailors aboard too benumbed to adjust it, sent Surfmen Randall and Amazeen back to the rock to see if there were any more men on the wreck. A big wave carried both surfmen off their feet; but Amazeen seized Randall as the sea rolled back, and clung with him to the rock. The rest of the crew dashed out to their rescue; but they were saved only just in time, for they were almost exhausted when brought ashore.

The rescue of these shipwrecked sailors was surrounded by most perilous circumstances; for while Keeper Harding and his

men were engaged in saving the crew of the *Dyer*, they were, in turn, engaged in saving one another.

To no life-saving crew does the term « heroes of peace » more exactly apply than to that of the station at Evanston, Illinois, on Lake Michigan. With the exception of the keeper, it is composed of students of the Northwestern University, who, when not on duty at the station, are quietly pursuing their studies. It is a kind of college team that has the waves of Lake Michigan for a playground, human lives for a goal, and the elements for umpire.

One Thanksgiving morning these brave fellows received word that the life was being pounded out of a steamer and her crew off Fort Sheridan, twelve miles distant. With the life-boat they made their way to the scene of the disaster. From the bluff they could see the vessel in the breakers, about a thousand yards from shore. There was a living gale, the thermometer was below the freezing-point, and the air thick with snow and sleet.

A wild ravine—a roaring, ice-glazed crack in the bluff—led down to the shore. It would have been impossible even for this plucky crew to have taken the boat safely down through the steep ravine; but soldiers and civilians, armed with picks and shovels, hewed out steps from its side, and mowed a path through the brush. The beach was a mere strip, exposed to the full fury of the sheeting waves. Thrice, in hauling the boat to the windward point, from which Keeper Lawson decided to launch, it filled.

The bluff was lined with soldiers and others from the fort, and every one held his breath as the frail-looking boat, which seemed a mere cockle-shell amid the writhing waters, left the beach. Once it nearly pitch-poled; once it filled to the thwarts; and though the crew pulled with the strength of desperation, it was driven to leeward, and had to be forced toward the wreck in the very teeth of the gale. The life-savers' clothing was frozen stiff; the vessel was shrouded with ice; her crew, half perished, huddled forward. At last the boat was forced under the steamer's lee, and six men were brought off and taken ashore. Three trips were made in all, and when the life-savers finally beached their boat, their condition was almost as pitiable as that of those they had saved. That was this college team's Thanksgiving game. They won it against fearful odds, a fact attested by the gold medals awarded to keeper and crew: Lawrence O. Lawson, George Crosby,

William M. Ewing, Jacob Loining, Edson B. Fowler, William L. Wilson, and Frank M. Kindig.

To me the rescue of the crew of the British schooner *H. P. Kirkham*, by the crew of the Coskata life-saving station, Nantucket Island, seems the most daring exploit ever performed within the scope of the service. Twenty-six hours elapsed between the time the life-boat was launched and its landing with the crew of the wrecked vessel—twenty-six hours of exposure in an open boat, amid the tide-rips and riotous cross-seas of the Nantucket shoals.

An overcast sky, with occasional snow-squalls, the thermometer twenty degrees below the freezing-point, an icy norther whistling over the sand-dunes—such was the night preceding this rescue.

The Coskata patrols went over their dreary beats, returning to the station chilled and worn with their long trudge through the heavy snow and sand.

At daybreak wind and sea were still rising. Keeper Chase carefully swept with his long glass as much of the coast as he could bring within range; but no vessel was visible. Just then there was a ring at the station telephone, and the lighthouse-keeper at Sankaty Head reported that, just before dawn, he had seen torch-flashes offshore, and thought he could discern the masts of a vessel on Bass Rip, ten miles out. Keeper Chase again made a careful search. There was no vessel in sight. She must be outside even of Bass Rip. The crew was quickly mustered, and Sankaty Head was called up.

« Is the vessel still there? »

« Yes; still there.»

« All right. We will launch and go to her at once. Call up Vineyard Haven, and, if there's a tug in port, ask the master to run off toward Great Rip. Tell him a vessel somewhere beyond there may need a tug; that we 've gone out to her; and that, if he can't render assistance to her, we 'll probably need him to get back against wind and sea.»

Not a man of the crew but knew what it meant to run before a gale on Nantucket Shoals. The gale must moderate, some vessel must pick them up, or seven more men would share the fate of those on the wreck. These descendants of old-time whalemen had no need to speak of this to one another. With the fathers it had been, « Dead whale, or stove boat »; with the sons it was, « Rescued crew, or drowned life-savers.»

Sail was made, and Bass Rip reached in a comparatively short time. From there the vessel was first seen, five miles farther out. « On the Rose and Crown Shoal! » exclaimed Keeper Chase. This is the most dangerous of the numerous outlying shoals; but, nothing daunted, the keeper headed the boat for it. When the life-savers got near enough they could make out seven men clinging to the rigging of a three-masted schooner, the hull of which had already worked itself so deep into the treacherous shoal that only part of the port rail could be seen. The sea broke high over the bow, and swirled over deck and stern.

The life-boat was anchored, a hawser taken over the bow, and, carefully steadied by the oars and the long steering-sweep, the boat dropped down with the current toward the wreck, the life-savers intent upon the keeper's every command, whether by word or gesture. One misstroke might mean failure and death. Carefully working in between seas, it became at last possible to hurl a heaving-stick with a small line attached into the rigging. A heavier line was « bent » on to the stick by the schooner's crew, drawn aboard the life-boat, and made fast to the after thwart; and then two of the boat's crew began to haul in carefully toward the wreck.

And now occurred one of the dramatic incidents of the rescue. The half-frenzied sailors, intent only upon saving their own lives, began hauling rapidly on their end of the line, at the imminent danger of swamping the life-boat.

« Make that line fast! » shouted Keeper Chase. But the schooner's crew was demoralized and undisciplined, and no attention was paid to the command.

Keeper Chase passed his knife to the stroke-oarsman. « I have charge here,» he shouted. « Pull this boat another foot nearer that wreck, and the line shall be cut! »

Keeper Chase stands six feet four inches in his boots, and he has a six-foot-four-inch voice. He towered above the seas in the eyes of the shipwrecked crew, and his command rang in their ears above the storm; and there stood the stroke-oarsman, knife in hand, ready to sever the line. The little wave-tossed boat at the end of that line was their only hope of safety; and so they made fast, and the life-savers worked in as close to the wreck as caution would permit. One after another, the seven men were taken off the wreck, where for fifteen hours almost certain death had been staring them in the face.

Keeper Chase knew that the rescued men, hungry, cold, and exhausted with their long night struggle, drenched with icy seas, and pierced with the north wind, were worse than useless—mere dead weight in the boat. In fact, it would be little less than a miracle if they reached shore alive. So they were simply stowed away lengthwise in the bottom of the boat. From the deeply laden craft no land could be seen. Only the tall red-and-white tower on Sankaty, Nantucket's boldest headland, was now and then barely discernible as the boat rose on the crest of a high sea.

Mast and sail, useless now against a head wind and sea, were cast overboard. The anchor was lifted, and the boat headed shoreward. Wind and current combined to force it toward the breaking shoal, which was weathered only after three hours of the hardest pulling. It was impossible to make further headway at that time, and the boat was again anchored, to await the turn of the tide, which might aid in reaching land.

At sunset, six hours after leaving the wreck (which had split up an hour after the rescue), the boat had made only one mile of the fifteen toward shore. To be at anchor in such seas meant no rest. Rolling and pitching, the boat was shipping water with almost every wave, and the utmost exertion was required to keep it even comparatively free. The southern tide was due at 9 P. M., but the fierce norther had caused such a set that, after an hour's pull, the crew was obliged to anchor again. The rescued men weighted the boat and added to the danger of swamping; one of them was moaning piteously; and the bow-oarsman of the rescuing crew was also overcome for a while.

At last one of the life-savers, Perkins, or, as his boat-mates called him, « Perkie,» said, « Captain, let me sleep ten minutes, and I 'll be all right.» So the members of the crew were allowed to sleep in turn, but only a few minutes at a time, for fear of freezing.

The boat had been launched at eight o'clock one morning; it was three o'clock of the next. At last the southern tide made up, wind and sea moderated somewhat, and with sunrise another pull was made for shore. At ten o'clock, twenty-six. hours after the crew had left Coskata, they beached the boat at Siasconset, on the southeastern shore of Nantucket, some eight miles across the island from the station, to which they were too exhausted to return until the afternoon.

When the crew started from Coskata, they left behind them in the station a woman, Keeper Chase's wife. As hour after hour wore away, she watched and waited, hoping against hope. When the crew reached the station, she came out, stood up on tiptoe, drew the keeper's bearded face down to hers, and kissed him.

There are times when the tension upon the emotions is so great that the least giving way results in a total collapse; and perhaps this is the reason Keeper Chase—his voice a bit husky, it is true—merely turned to his crew and called out:

« Now, boys, stow away the boat, and get your suppers. It 's 'most time for the sunset patrol to be out.» And so the routine was quietly resumed.

From the time the life-boat left the wreck until at sunrise the next morning the imperiled life-savers had kept a constant lookout for any tug that might have put out to their aid from Vineyard Haven. Did a tug start in response to the message from Sankaty? Yes; it stood offshore some five or six miles, and then, afraid to proceed farther in such seas and gale, ran for shelter!

The medals which were awarded to this valiant crew arrived too late for one of its members, the cheerful « Perkie.» He had been weakened by an attack of pneumonia the previous winter, and the exposure of those terrible twenty-six hours brought on consumption. He knew the medals had been awarded; and when the keeper visited him shortly before his death, he asked, « Captain, have n't those stove-covers come yet?»

« Perkie » was the sole joy and support of an aged mother, and the medal which came too late for him is the only consolation of this poor sorrowing soul.

A number of other crews in the life-saving service have received medals for heroic rescues. The crew of the Hog Island, Virginia, station were awarded medals, not only by our government, but also by Spain, for saving nineteen men from the Spanish steamer *San Albano*. Two daring attempts with the surf-boat having failed, Keeper Johnson most ingeniously ran his gun-cart far into the surf in the wake of a receding wave, and before the next sea boomed in quickly shot a line out to the wreck, and scrambled back to the beach. Christopher Ludlam and his crew were decorated for rescuing in their surf-boat, during a heavy northeast gale and snow-storm, the crew of the lime-schooner *D. H. Ingraham*, stranded and afire among the breakers on the bar at Hereford Inlet, New Jersey; John C. Patterson and his crew, of the Shark River, New Jersey, station, for a rescue effected during a heavy onshore gale—the keeper, as he stood, his hand on the gunwale, ready to make the launch, receiving a summons to a brother's death-bed, notwithstanding which, he, with pale, determined face, gave the order to «shove her in»; Keepers Benjamin B. Dailey of the Cape Hatteras, and Patrick H. Etheridge of the Creed's Hill station, adjoining, and six surfmen from the former, for saving the crew of the barkentine *Ephraim Williams*, a five-mile pull in a wintry gale, the boat, in passing through the second line of breakers, rising so sheer that the whole inside was visible from shore, and the little craft seemed about to fall over backward; Keeper C. C. Goodwin of the Cleveland, Ohio, station, and his crew, for rescuing within eleven days, during gales and in freezing weather, twenty-nine lives from three vessels; Keeper Chadwick and his crew of the Mantoloking, New Jersey, station, and five volunteers, for remarkable skill and endurance in the rescue of the crew of the schooner *George Taulane;* and Keeper Charles H. Valentine and his crew, of the Monmouth Beach, New Jersey, station, for rescuing the crews of two vessels, the second rescue being effected through what was a hand-to-hand fight with the surf and the wreckage from the first vessel. Some fishermen formed what was literally a life-line, reaching from the beach into the surf by locking hands, and thus assisted in the rescue.

The award of medals was authorized in 1874. Almost the first award was made to two English life-saving crews for the rescue of the crew of an American ship wrecked at the mouth of the Mersey—an act of recognition pleasantly matched by that of Spain in decorating the rescuers of the *San Albano's* crew.

During the session of 1894–95 the New York legislature passed resolutions praising in the highest terms the heroism of several life-saving crews on Long Island, among them that of the Lone Hill station.

«Lone Hill!» What a dreary name, suggestive of a wind-swept sand-dune rising in desolate isolation from a sea-worn beach! No wonder the disaster, in spite of the heroism it called forth, has lineaments as terrible as storm and death can present. It combines with a marvelous exhibition of endurance and courage, not only on the part of the life-savers, but also on the part of one of the sailors of the ill-fated vessel, the most tragic aspects of shipwreck. After a forty-four hours' fight for life, only two survivors of a crew of eight were brought ashore, and of these two, one died soon afterward. That

he reached shore with a spark of life in him was due to the almost superhuman efforts of his shipmate, who, with death staring him in the face, and at a time when self-preservation would have been uppermost in the mind of almost any one, watched over this unfortunate with a care, tenderness, and devotion bordering on the miraculous. Yet he was only a common sailor; and when he himself had recovered from the effects of that winter storm, quietly went his way, and is probably still before the mast.

It is needless to follow the three-masted schooner *Louis V. Place* through all the stress of winter weather which she encountered after she weighed from Baltimore on her last voyage. It converted the vessel into little more than a drifting iceberg. Her running-gear was frozen in the blocks, her sails were as stiff as boards, her decks sheeted with ice. On the morning that was to be her last, the captain, her whereabouts being wholly a matter of conjecture (he thought he was off Sandy Hook), tried to let go his anchors in hope of holding her off the lee shore which his soundings told him was near. But the crew, already subjected to four days and nights of bitter exposure, failed in their efforts to clear away the ice-bound anchors. Though the halyards were cut, the sails, rigid with ice, remained upright in their places, and the vessel's course landward was unchecked. When the shock came—the shock a vessel feels but once—all hands took to the mizzen-rigging.

The men of the Lone Hill station, eight miles east of Fire Island light, were returning from the rescue of a shipwrecked crew when they were notified that a vessel had just stranded near their station. They were soon abreast of her. She lay some four hundred yards out, swept from end to end by the waves. Frequent snow-squalls obscured the atmosphere; the surf was full of porridge ice, and great cakes of ice were piled up on the beach. To launch, let alone pull, a boat under such conditions was beyond human strength. While the Lyle gun was being made ready, two of the men in the rigging were seen to let go their hold and drop into the sea. This occurrence, so early in the catastrophe, was appalling evidence that the crew's vitality was at a low ebb, and that succor, to be of much avail, must be immediate.

It was only at intervals between the snow gusts that the gun could be fired. The second shot landed the line over the rigging, almost within grasp of the shipwrecked sailors; but not one of them stirred to reach for it. By one o'clock in the afternoon four lines had been fired; but it was evident that the crew was too exhausted or too nearly dead to aid in its own rescue.

The weather now closed in so thick that the vessel was invisible for three hours. Then a glimpse of a few minutes disclosed only four instead of six figures in the rigging. Two had silently frozen and dropped into the sea. Twice more the gun was fired, but again without avail. Darkness now set in. It was a wild, pitiless night. The life-savers built a beacon fire, and watched the surf for any chance, however desperate, to launch their boat. None came, and with daybreak, almost twenty-four hours after the vessel had stranded, it was seen that of the four figures in the rigging only two showed signs of life.

It had been evident already the previous day, and became more so on this, that one of these, if he survived, would owe his life to his shipmate, who, during these awful hours, instead of concentrating his efforts upon his own preservation, made every endeavor to keep up the feeble vitality in the other, beating him with the end of a rope, and shaking and pounding him, in turn. The mizzenmast seemed to be growing insecure; and at low tide, when part of the vessel's deck was not awash, this man slowly and painfully made his way down to it and along it to the main rigging. But before going up he turned and looked at the man he had left in the mizzen. Tottering back, and groping his way up until he reached him again, he in some miraculous way brought him down to the deck, and, by shoving and dragging him, got him over to the main rigging and up it. That the two other figures on the wreck were only frozen corpses soon became apparent. When the sailor who would not desert his shipmate, evidently with the intention of lashing him fast, unwound some rope near these figures, they were suddenly loosened, and swung, one by the head, the other by the feet, to and fro in the gale, nearly knocking the two survivors out of the rigging.

The second day was now rapidly waning. The ninth and last shot was fired. It laid the line fair across the hull, between the main- and fore-mast. The watchers held their breath as the sailor who had shown such unexpected vitality slowly came out of the rigging. He bent over stiffly and painfully, picked up the line, made an effort as if to haul, staggered, fell, and crept feebly back to the rigging. The tension among those

ashore had been so great that, when this seemingly last hope of saving what little of life remained on the doomed ship failed, three of the men burst into tears.

During the waning hours of that second day, and even in the gathering darkness, desperate, almost frantic efforts were made to launch the surf-boat. Each time it was simply tossed back upon the ice-rimmed beach. Again a fire was built, and again the surf watched, as it rushed into the glare, for a favorable opportunity for action. At last, almost at midnight, more than forty hours after the vessel had stranded, the surf seemed a little less powerful and the ice less densely packed. This was the supreme moment. With a mighty rush, the boat was sent into the surf. Waves breasted her, ice pounded her; but, driven on with all the strength her resolute crew could gather, she was at last laid alongside the storm-swept hulk, and the two perishing men were taken off. It was one o'clock on the morning of the third day when they were borne into the Lone Hill station. The heroic sailor, William Stevens, who had done all he could to save his shipmate, recovered. The latter's condition was so pitiable as to beggar description. His feet were frozen solid in his boots. Amputation became necessary, and he died at the hospital to which, at the earliest possible moment, he had been taken from the station.

This gallant rescue was accomplished by Keeper Baker of Lone Hill, Keeper Rorke of Blue Point, and five surfmen. As the resolution passed by the New York legislature says, «Such a service belongs to humanity, and deserves universal admiration.» True; but true also of William Stevens of the fo'c'sle.

Heroism in the life-saving service is not confined to any one part of our coast. Crews along the Atlantic, as well as on the Lakes, hold medals; and Joseph Napier and Ingar Oleson, members of Lake crews, have been similarly honored for individual daring. The Pacific coast also has its heroes in the service, among them John Regnier, who, while engaged with his crew in a rescue on Humboldt Bay, California, sprang into the surf and recovered a child whom the boat had twice failed to reach—a deed for which he holds the gold medal.

There may be, in the record of the life-saving service, instances of failure through lack of judgment, but none through shirking. On the contrary, the occasions when chances too desperate have been taken have been almost too frequent. Crew after crew has calmly gone to its death rather than give quibbling critics of the service the slightest chance to question its spirit. One winter night the Barnegat life-savers launched their boat, and disappeared into the storm and the darkness, never again to be seen alive. The wiping out of the Point aux Barques crew has already been related. Such instances are not isolated. Hardly a season passes without adding its tribute of lives sacrificed to the honor-roll of the service.

Circumstances singularly pathetic surround the loss which befell the crew of the Peaked Hill station, near Provincetown, Cape Cod. Keeper Atkins of this station was one of the true and trusted veterans of the service. But one stormy day in winter, after twelve hours' exposure on the beach, exhausted by futile efforts to launch the surf-boat, he and his crew had the mortification of seeing the rescue they had attempted made by a crew of volunteers. It mattered not that these had made no previous exertions, that they had come fresh and unwearied upon the scene; Keeper Atkins and his crew had to take from the community what, in the staid, old-fashioned speech of the Cape, is known as the «goading slur.»

The keeper made no attempt to answer his critics; but gradually, as that season and the following summer wore away, a settled look of determination became stamped on his face, and his bearing took on a dignity almost tragic. When, at the opening of the next season, his wife, as he left his home for the station, begged him not to expose himself to needless danger, he replied:

«Before this season is over I will have wiped out the ‹goading slur.›»

Reaching the station, he called his crew about him, and informed them that, no matter at what peril, a rescue would be attempted at every wreck within the limits of the station.

That winter a storm of almost unprecedented fury burst over the coast, and a vessel was swept upon the Peaked Hill bars. A surf-boat, launched by seemingly superhuman power, put out from shore. But neither desperation, nor even madness, could keep a boat afloat in such a sea; and when, one after another, those who had braved it were cast upon the beach, three were dead. One of these was Keeper Atkins. He had wiped out the «goading slur.»

Of such stuff are the heroes of the life-saving service.

About the Author

PAUL GIAMBARBA began his career as a copy boy with the *Boston Post*. He was also a sports cartoonist for the *Boston Herald*, a contributor to *True, Sports Illustrated*, and a weekly contributor to *This Week* and two *Scholastic Magazines*. In 1965 he began The Scrimshaw Press in an effort to make available abundantly illustrated original material in paperback form at modest prices. Books from The Scrimshaw Press have been reviewed by *Scientific American, The Boston Globe, American Artist, National Fisherman, Library Journal, School Library Journal, Horn Book* and *Scholastic Teacher*. Articles about The Scrimshaw Press have appeared in *American Artist* and *Horn Book*. Atlantic/Little, Brown published *The Lighthouse at Dangerfield*, a book about Highland Light on Cape Cod by Paul Giambarba, in 1969.